D0477282

EGMONT

We bring stories to life

First published in Great Britain 2017, by Egmont UK Limited
The Yellow Building, 1 Nicholas Road
London W11 4AN

Written by Stephanie Milton
Additional material by Owen Jones and Marsh Davies
Designed by Andrea Philpots, Joe Bolder and John Stuckey
Illustrations by Ryan Marsh and James Bale
Cover designed by John Stuckey
Production by Louis Harvey
Special thanks to Lydia Winters, Owen Jones, Junkboy,
Martin Johansson, Marsh Davies and Jesper Öqvist.

© 2017 Mojang AB and Mojang Synergies AB. MINECRAFT is a trademark or registered trademark of Mojang Synergies AB.

All rights reserved.

ISBN 978 1 4052 8599 5

66812/1
Printed in EU

ONLINE SAFETY FOR YOUNGER FANS

Spending time online is great fun! Here are a few simple rules to help younger fans stay safe and keep the internet a great place to spend time:

- Never give out your real name – don't use it as your username.
- Never give out any of your personal details.
- Never tell anybody which school you go to or how old you are.
- Never tell anybody your password except a parent or a guardian.
- Be aware that you must be 13 or over to create an account on many sites. Always check the site policy and ask a parent or guardian for permission before registering.
- Always tell a parent or guardian if something is worrying you.

Stay safe online. Any website addresses listed in this book are correct at the time of going to print. However, Egmont is not responsible for content hosted by third parties. Please be aware that online content can be subject to change and websites can contain content that is unsuitable for children. We advise that all children are supervised when using the internet.

GUIDE TO:

 **THE NETHER & THE END**

CONTENTS

1. THE NETHER

2. THE END

INTRODUCTION

Welcome, bold adventurers, clever crafters and worldly wanderers! Are you ready for an even greater challenge, with even greater rewards, than anything found in the grassy plains and craggy mountains of Minecraft's Overworld? You soon will be! In these pages we'll dig through the secrets of the Nether – a place of roiling lava lakes and black caverns – and the strange reality of the End, with its pale islands, floating in an inky void. Ghasts! Shulkers! Such foes you will learn to face as you conquer the furthest reaches of the world. So, be sure to pack this book before stepping through a portal – and good luck!

MARSH DAVIES
THE MOJANG TEAM

KEY

Throughout the pages of this book you'll see symbols that represent different items, values or properties. Refer back to this page when you spot them to check what they mean.

GENERAL

MOJANG STUFF

This super-exclusive info has come directly from the developers at Mojang.

SPAWN LIGHT LEVEL

15

9

0

Indicates the light level at which a mob spawns. In this example, the mob spawns at a light level of 9 or higher.

HOSTILITY

Indicates the hostility level of a mob – yellow is passive, orange is neutral and red is hostile.

	Block projectiles with your shield		Drink a potion of strength		Shoot with enchanted bow and arrows
	Block projectiles with your sword		Get yourself into a two block-high space and hit the mob's legs		Stand on two block-high tower and hit them with a sword
	Disable mob spawner with 5 torches		Hit with enchanted diamond sword		Stand on a three block-high tower and hit them with a sword
	Drink a potion of fire resistance		Pelt with snowballs		Throw a splash potion of healing at it
	Drink a potion of healing		Reel in with fishing rod		Use a bed then step backwards quickly to avoid the explosion

	Blaze powder
	Blaze rod
	Bones
	Bowl
	Coal
	Cobblestone
	Cocoa beans
	Diamond
	Dragon egg
	Egg
	Ender pearl
	Experience point
	Eye of ender
	Feather
	Flint
	Ghast tear

	Glass
	Glowstone dust
	Gold ingot
	Gold nugget
	Gold sword
	Gunpowder
	Iron ingot
	Magma cream
	Milk
	Mushroom (brown)
	Mushroom (red)
	Nether brick
	Nether quartz
	Nether star
	Obsidian
	Popped chorus fruit

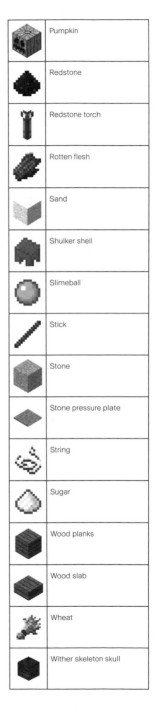

	Pumpkin
	Redstone
	Redstone torch
	Rotten flesh
	Sand
	Shulker shell
	Slimeball
	Stick
	Stone
	Stone pressure plate
	String
	Sugar
	Wood planks
	Wood slab
	Wheat
	Wither skeleton skull

THE NETHER

After the rolling green hills and lush forests of the Overworld, the Nether is a dramatic change of scene. In this section you'll discover what awaits you on the other side of your Nether portal, how to defeat the Nether's hellish hostile mobs and where to look for valuable blocks and items.

THE NETHER ENVIRONMENT

The perilous Nether dimension is partially submerged in lava and inhabited by five dangerous hostile mobs that you won't have seen before. It's also home to many useful materials that are essential to your progress. Let's take a look at the environment.

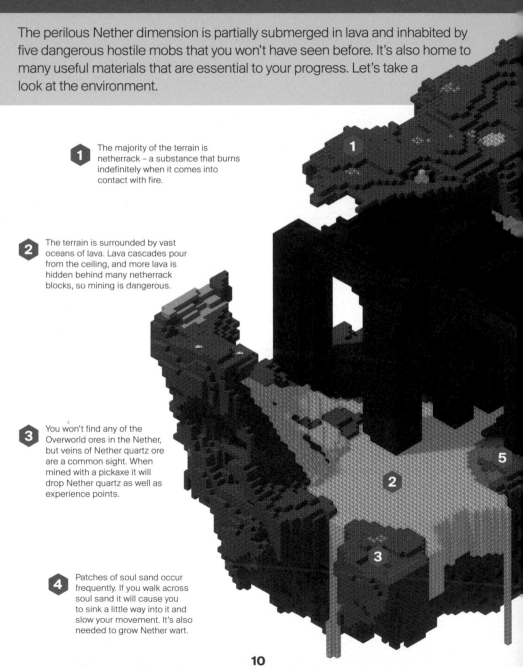

1 The majority of the terrain is netherrack – a substance that burns indefinitely when it comes into contact with fire.

2 The terrain is surrounded by vast oceans of lava. Lava cascades pour from the ceiling, and more lava is hidden behind many netherrack blocks, so mining is dangerous.

3 You won't find any of the Overworld ores in the Nether, but veins of Nether quartz ore are a common sight. When mined with a pickaxe it will drop Nether quartz as well as experience points.

4 Patches of soul sand occur frequently. If you walk across soul sand it will cause you to sink a little way into it and slow your movement. It's also needed to grow Nether wart.

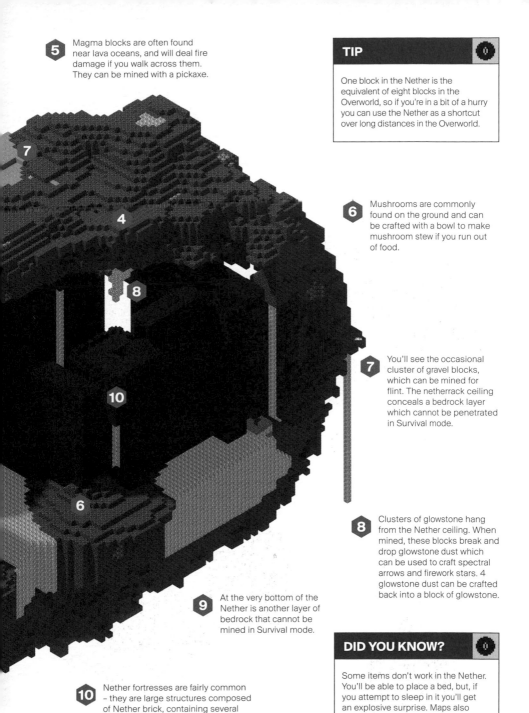

5 Magma blocks are often found near lava oceans, and will deal fire damage if you walk across them. They can be mined with a pickaxe.

TIP

One block in the Nether is the equivalent of eight blocks in the Overworld, so if you're in a bit of a hurry you can use the Nether as a shortcut over long distances in the Overworld.

6 Mushrooms are commonly found on the ground and can be crafted with a bowl to make mushroom stew if you run out of food.

7 You'll see the occasional cluster of gravel blocks, which can be mined for flint. The netherrack ceiling conceals a bedrock layer which cannot be penetrated in Survival mode.

8 Clusters of glowstone hang from the Nether ceiling. When mined, these blocks break and drop glowstone dust which can be used to craft spectral arrows and firework stars. 4 glowstone dust can be crafted back into a block of glowstone.

9 At the very bottom of the Nether is another layer of bedrock that cannot be mined in Survival mode.

DID YOU KNOW?

Some items don't work in the Nether. You'll be able to place a bed, but, if you attempt to sleep in it you'll get an explosive surprise. Maps also don't work, and you can't place water anywhere except in a cauldron.

10 Nether fortresses are fairly common – they are large structures composed of Nether brick, containing several interesting features including loot chests and blaze spawners. See pages 34-35 for more info on Nether fortresses.

NETHER BLOCKS AND THEIR USES

If you're skilled enough to navigate the Nether's many dangers and collect the unique materials found there, a host of new crafting recipes will become available to you. Here are some examples of how you can put your Nether spoils to good use back in the Overworld.

NETHERRACK
Due to its ability to burn indefinitely, netherrack can be used to make fireplaces. You can also use it on perimeter walls to deter enemy players from raiding your base.

GLOWSTONE
Glowstone has a luminance of 15 – the highest possible light level – so it's an ideal block to use in light fixtures.

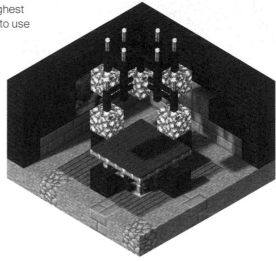

SOUL SAND

Soul sand can be used to make endermite and silverfish traps. Due to their small size, both mobs will suffocate in it. Soul sand is also used to grow Nether wart – an important potion ingredient – and is necessary to craft the wither, one of Minecraft's boss mobs.

NETHER BRICK

Nether brick has the same blast resistance as cobblestone but looks much more polished and dramatic. It's an excellent construction material for bases.

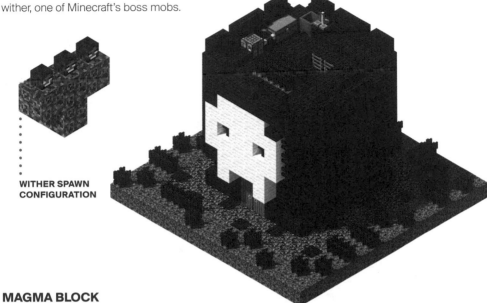

WITHER SPAWN CONFIGURATION

MAGMA BLOCK

Since magma blocks deal fire damage and Overworld mobs are not immune, they are ideal for use in Overworld base defences and traps.

NETHER QUARTZ

Nether quartz is a key ingredient in several redstone crafting recipes, and can be combined into decorative blocks of quartz for use in construction. A block of quartz only has a blast resistance of 4 (compared to cobblestone and Nether brick, which have a blast resistance of 30) so it's best used for base details rather than entire builds.

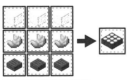

DAYLIGHT SENSOR RECIPE

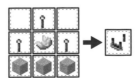

REDSTONE COMPARATOR RECIPE

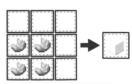

QUARTZ BLOCK RECIPE

PREPARING FOR A TRIP TO THE NETHER

So you've convinced yourself that a trip to the Nether is necessary. But if you want to make it back alive with an inventory full of useful supplies, you'll need to arm yourself with the right equipment. Here's a definitive guide to what you'll need to take with you.

WEAPONS AND DEFENSIVE ITEMS

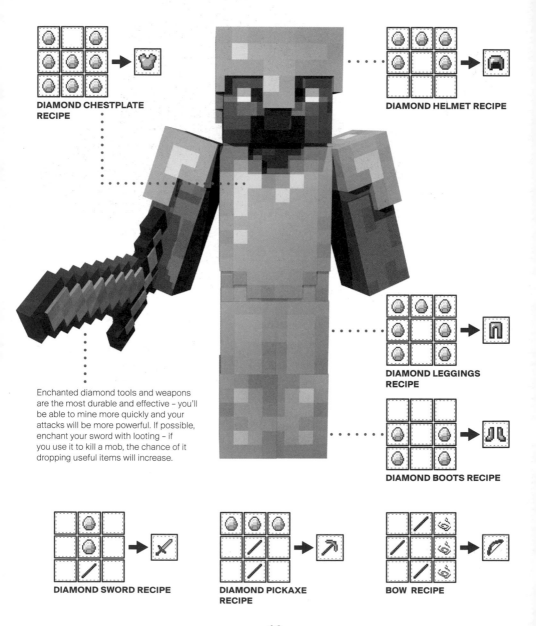

DIAMOND CHESTPLATE RECIPE

DIAMOND HELMET RECIPE

DIAMOND LEGGINGS RECIPE

DIAMOND BOOTS RECIPE

Enchanted diamond tools and weapons are the most durable and effective – you'll be able to mine more quickly and your attacks will be more powerful. If possible, enchant your sword with looting – if you use it to kill a mob, the chance of it dropping useful items will increase.

DIAMOND SWORD RECIPE

DIAMOND PICKAXE RECIPE

BOW RECIPE

Snowballs are essential for blaze combat as they deal 3 damage per hit. Breaking snow blocks with a shovel will give you snowballs.

Drinking helpful potions will counteract the damage you take and keep your health up – fire resistance and healing potions are ideal but you'll need to be set up for brewing first. Witches sometimes drop potions when defeated.

You'll be safest in enchanted diamond armour. Fire protection and blast protection enchantments will come in particularly handy.

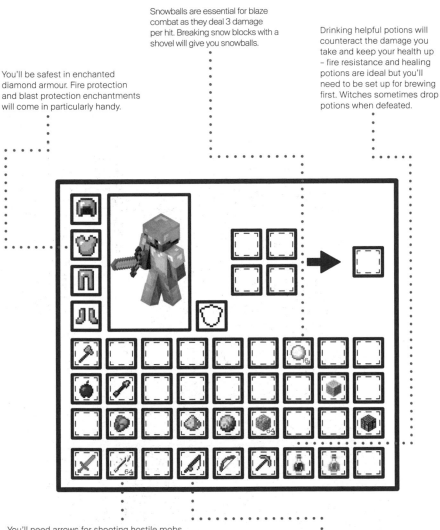

You'll need arrows for shooting hostile mobs from a safe distance. Tipped arrows are best, but you'll need lingering potions to make them, which involves combining a potion with dragon's breath.

A fishing rod will come in handy for fighting ghasts. See pages 24-25 for more info.

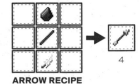

ARROW RECIPE

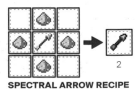

SPECTRAL ARROW RECIPE

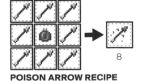

POISON ARROW RECIPE

15

OTHER TOOLS AND BLOCKS

1 The chance of your Nether portal being damaged by ghast fireballs is extremely high. Make sure you have spare obsidian blocks to rebuild it and a flint and steel to relight it.

LADDER RECIPE

2 Ladders will help you to navigate the Nether's many cliffs more safely.

3 Wood doesn't generate naturally in the Nether, so take a stack of unrefined wood for crafting replacement tools and weapons.

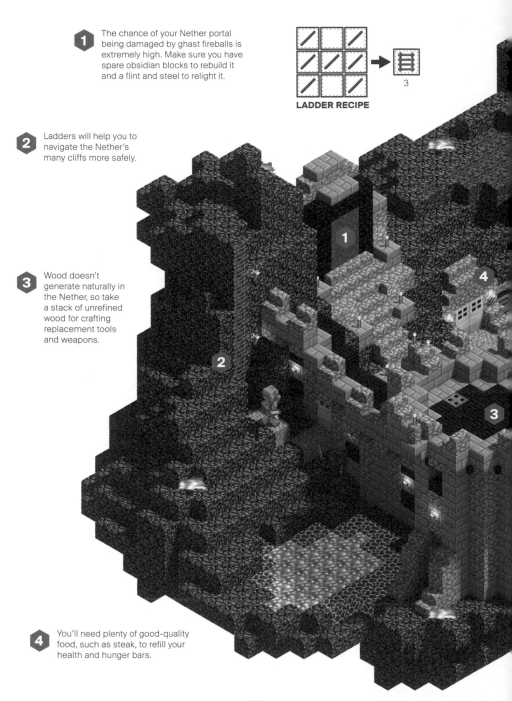

4 You'll need plenty of good-quality food, such as steak, to refill your health and hunger bars.

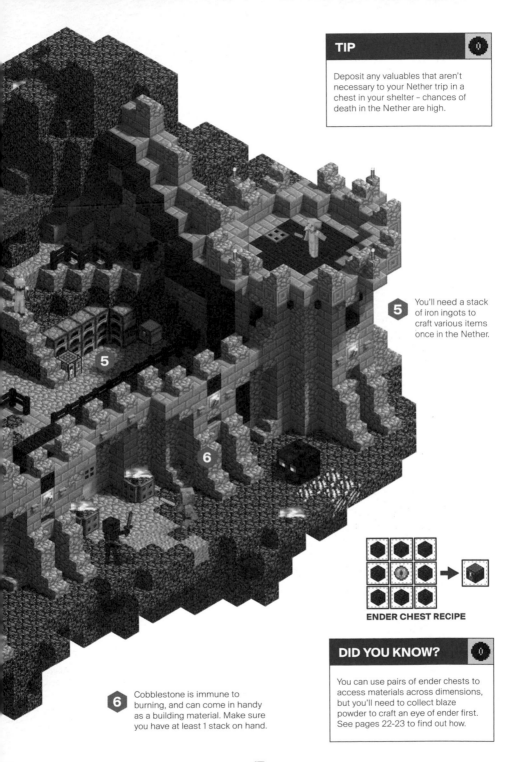

TIP

Deposit any valuables that aren't
necessary to your Nether trip in a
chest in your shelter – chances of
death in the Nether are high.

5 You'll need a stack
of iron ingots to
craft various items
once in the Nether.

ENDER CHEST RECIPE

6 Cobblestone is immune to
burning, and can come in handy
as a building material. Make sure
you have at least 1 stack on hand.

DID YOU KNOW?

You can use pairs of ender chests to
access materials across dimensions,
but you'll need to collect blaze
powder to craft an eye of ender first.
See pages 22-23 to find out how.

NETHER PORTALS

There is no naturally-occuring gateway between the Overworld and the Nether – you'll need to build a Nether portal. This portal enables you to travel back and forth between the two dimensions, as long as it remains activated. Let's look at how to create a standard Nether portal using the minimum number of obsidian blocks.

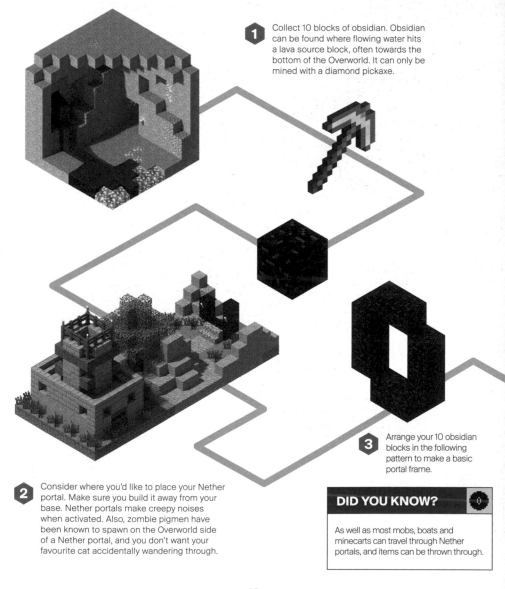

1 Collect 10 blocks of obsidian. Obsidian can be found where flowing water hits a lava source block, often towards the bottom of the Overworld. It can only be mined with a diamond pickaxe.

3 Arrange your 10 obsidian blocks in the following pattern to make a basic portal frame.

2 Consider where you'd like to place your Nether portal. Make sure you build it away from your base. Nether portals make creepy noises when activated. Also, zombie pigmen have been known to spawn on the Overworld side of a Nether portal, and you don't want your favourite cat accidentally wandering through.

DID YOU KNOW?

As well as most mobs, boats and minecarts can travel through Nether portals, and items can be thrown through.

Though for a long time Nether portals needed to be built to a very strict design, you can now make portals at larger sizes and different dimensions, just as long as it remains an oblong space enclosed in obsidian. Whatever shape and size you go for, though, the exit portal in the Nether is always generated at the default 4 x 5 scale. You can rebuild it, but be warned: unless the shapes on either end match, it can be tricky to work out where you'll emerge.

 7 Be very careful when exiting your portal on the Nether side. There's no way to control where it comes out, and if you're really unlucky it might be floating in mid-air over a sea of lava.

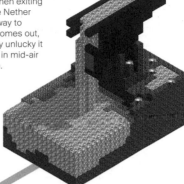

TIP

If you find that you've emerged on a floating island or over a lava ocean, try building out from the portal using cobblestone. Use the sneak function to ensure you don't fall over the edge.

 6 Stand in this vortex for 4 seconds and you'll be transported into the Nether.

4 If you'd prefer a proper rectangle you can also fill in the corners, but it'll work without them and save you 4 blocks of obsidian.

 5 Use a flint and steel on the space in the obsidian frame to activate the portal – portal blocks will appear.

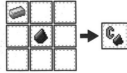

FLINT AND STEEL RECIPE

SURVIVAL AND EXPLORATION

Surviving in the Nether is no easy task. There's lava everywhere, treacherous cliffs to negotiate and terrifying new hostile mobs to deal with. Plus, the terrain doesn't have many distinguishing features so it's very easy to get lost. Follow these steps to give yourself the best chance of surviving as you explore.

1 Build a shelter around your portal. For now, make it out of cobblestone with an iron door – you can upgrade to Nether brick later. This will protect it from being destroyed by ghast fireballs and leaving you trapped in the Nether.

2 Once safely inside your portal shelter, take a moment to scan the area around you for immediate threats – mobs, lava streams, cliffs and magma blocks.

3 Make a crafting table and a chest for your shelter so that you're set up to make more equipment if necessary. Store some wood and iron ingots in here.

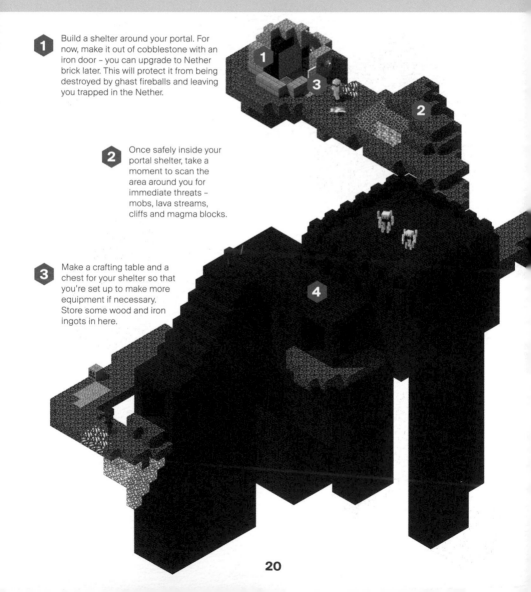

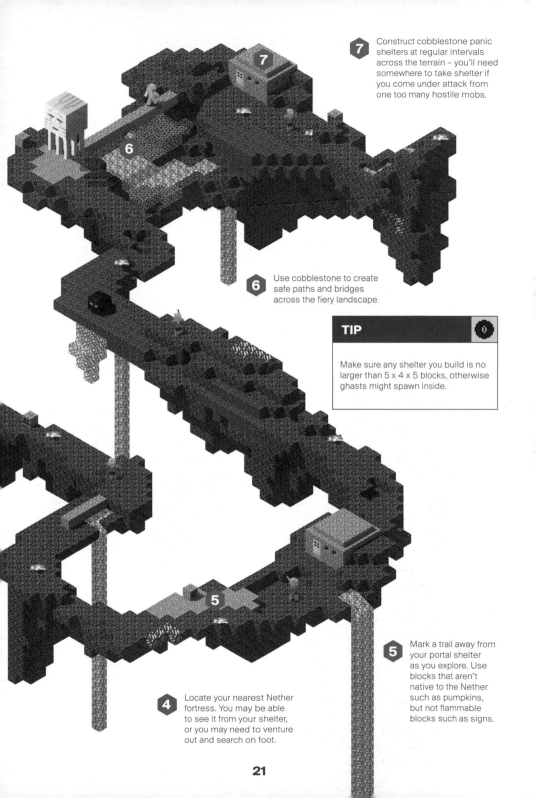

7 Construct cobblestone panic shelters at regular intervals across the terrain – you'll need somewhere to take shelter if you come under attack from one too many hostile mobs.

6 Use cobblestone to create safe paths and bridges across the fiery landscape.

TIP

Make sure any shelter you build is no larger than 5 x 4 x 5 blocks, otherwise ghasts might spawn inside.

5 Mark a trail away from your portal shelter as you explore. Use blocks that aren't native to the Nether such as pumpkins, but not flammable blocks such as signs.

4 Locate your nearest Nether fortress. You may be able to see it from your shelter, or you may need to venture out and search on foot.

NETHER MOBS

The Nether is crawling with powerful, flame-retardant hostile mobs and they do not appreciate you trespassing on their territory. Many can be found freely wandering the terrain, others prefer to stick to the Nether fortresses. Let's take a look at how they can be defeated and the useful items they might drop.

BLAZE

HEALTH POINTS		20
ATTACK STRENGTH		4-9
HOW TO DEFEAT		
ITEMS DROPPED		

0-1   10

SPAWN LIGHT LEVEL

15

11

0

SPAWN LOCATION
Anywhere in Nether fortresses, at light levels of 11 or lower and from monster spawners in the fortresses.

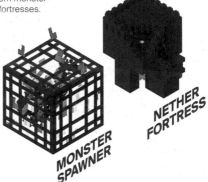

MONSTER SPAWNER

NETHER FORTRESS

BEHAVIOUR
Blazes hover just above the ground when idle, but will fly when whey find a target to attack. They produce smoke as they move, and blaze rods orbit their core. A metallic grinding noise will alert you to their presence.

ATTACK METHOD

Blazes pursue players within 48 blocks and shoot fireballs at their targets from up to 16 blocks away. These fireballs deal damage upon contact. Blazes will hit their targets when they are within 2 blocks of them, dealing damage.

SPECIAL SKILLS

Like all Nether mobs, blazes are immune to fire and lava so they have an immediate advantage. If they take damage from a player they will quickly alert all other blazes within 48 blocks, and they will all attack you in retaliation.

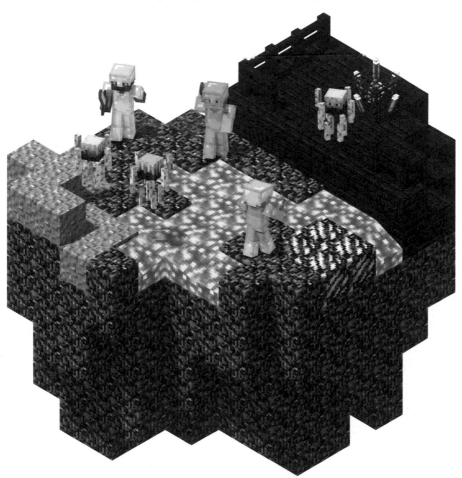

HOW TO DEFEAT

It's best to keep a safe distance when fighting a blaze. Throw snowballs at it to inflict damage, or shoot it with a bow and arrow. You should also drink a potion of fire resistance and try to disable the blaze spawner with five torches as soon as possible. If desperate, hit them with your sword.

USEFUL DROPS

Blazes may drop a blaze rod when defeated. Blaze rods are initially required to craft a brewing stand. They are also necessary to fuel the brewing stand but must be broken down into blaze powder first. Blaze powder is also needed to craft an eye of ender.

GHAST

HEALTH POINTS	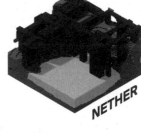 10
ATTACK STRENGTH	6-25
HOW TO DEFEAT	
ITEMS DROPPED	

0-2   0-1   5

15

SPAWN
LIGHT
LEVEL

0

**SPAWN
LOCATION** · · · · · · · · · · · · · · · · ·
Any 5 x 4 x 5 space in the
Nether at all light levels.

NETHER

BEHAVIOUR

Ghasts float slowly around the
Nether. When idle, their eyes and
mouth are closed as if they are
sleeping, but they are always on
the lookout for targets within 16
blocks. They make the occasional
strange, high-pitched sound.

ATTACK METHOD

You'll know a ghast is about to attack when it opens its red eyes and mouth. It makes a chirp-like sound when shooting fireballs. These fireballs have infinite range and deal damage upon contact with their target.

SPECIAL SKILLS

Ghasts are one of the largest mobs – their bodies are 4 x 4 x 4 blocks and they have 9 tentacles hanging from their underside. They also have an extremely long search radius and can target players from up to 100 blocks away.

DID YOU KNOW?

If you manage to destroy a ghast by deflecting its own fireball back at it, you'll earn the achievement Return to Sender.

HOW TO DEFEAT

If you have good aim, deflect the ghast's fireballs back at it with your sword. You can also shoot it from a distance with an enchanted bow and arrows, or reel it towards you on a fishing rod and finish it off with your sword.

USEFUL DROPS

Ghasts may drop up to 2 pieces of gunpowder, which is needed to craft TNT and fire charges. They may also drop a single ghast tear, which is needed to make mundane potion, potion of regeneration and End crystals.

MAGMA CUBE

HEALTH POINTS	1-16	
ATTACK STRENGTH	3-6	
HOW TO DEFEAT		
ITEMS DROPPED	0-1	1-4

15

**SPAWN
LIGHT
LEVEL**

0

DID YOU KNOW?

Magma cubes come in three delightful sizes: big, small and tiny. They all begin life as big magma cubes, but will divide into several smaller cubes when damaged, and then into several more tiny cubes before finally perishing.

BEHAVIOUR

Magma cubes can spawn anywhere in the Nether, but their spawn rate seems to be higher inside Nether fortresses. They bounce around when idle, searching for players to attack within a 16-block radius.

SPAWN
LOCATION · · · · · · · · · · · · · · ·
Anywhere in the Nether
at all light levels.

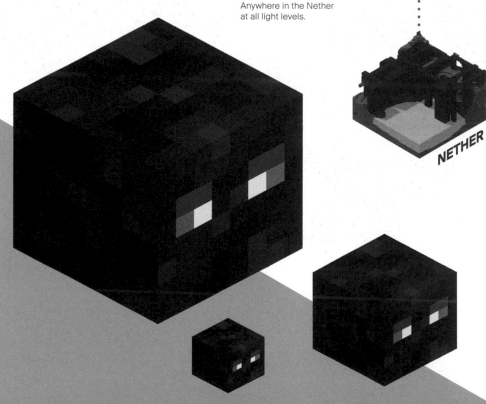

NETHER

ATTACK METHOD

You will take damage simply from touching a magma cube, but they bounce towards their target and attempt to land on top of it to deal the maximum amount of damage possible. As the magma cube divides into smaller cubes its jump strength decreases.

SPECIAL SKILLS

As well as being immune to burning in fire and lava, magma cubes are actually able to swim quite fast in lava. They are also immune to fall damage. When damaged they can divide into smaller cubes and can travel twice as fast as most other mobs.

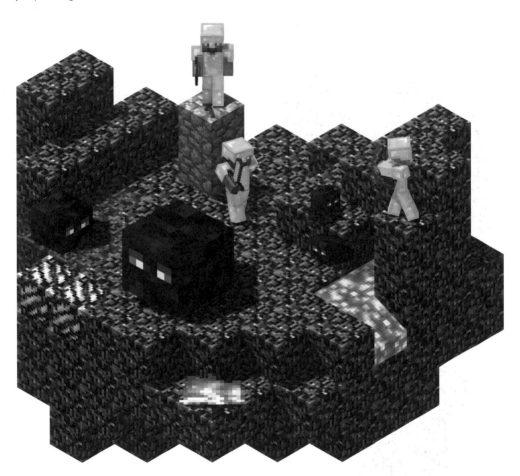

HOW TO DEFEAT

Stand on a two block-high pillar and hit the magma cube from above with a diamond sword. This will prevent them jumping on top of you. You can also shoot them from a safe distance with a bow and arrow.

USEFUL DROPS

Big and small magma cubes have a 25% chance of dropping 1 magma cream, but the chance increases if you use a looting sword. You need magma cream for mundane potion, potion of fire resistance and magma blocks.

WITHER SKELETON

HEALTH POINTS	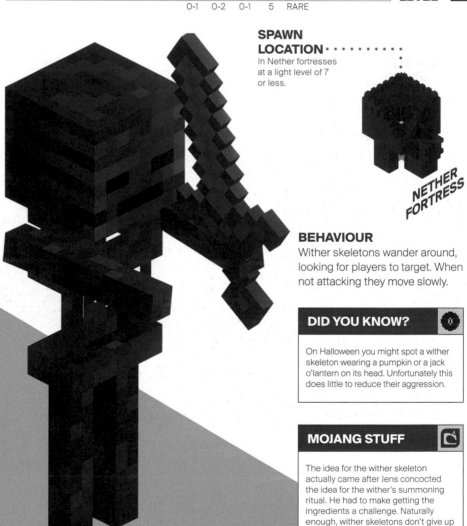 20	
ATTACK STRENGTH	4-10	
HOW TO DEFEAT		
ITEMS DROPPED		

0-1   0-2   0-1   5   RARE

SPAWN LIGHT LEVEL

15

7

0

SPAWN LOCATION · · · · · · · · · ·
In Nether fortresses at a light level of 7 or less.

NETHER FORTRESS

BEHAVIOUR
Wither skeletons wander around, looking for players to target. When not attacking they move slowly.

DID YOU KNOW?
On Halloween you might spot a wither skeleton wearing a pumpkin or a jack o'lantern on its head. Unfortunately this does little to reduce their aggression.

MOJANG STUFF
The idea for the wither skeleton actually came after Jens concocted the idea for the wither's summoning ritual. He had to make getting the ingredients a challenge. Naturally enough, wither skeletons don't give up their heads easily!

ATTACK METHOD

Wither skeletons sprint towards players and hit them with their stone sword on sight. They also inflict the wither effect for ten seconds. This effect turns the health bar black and drains it by 1 health point every 2 seconds.

SPECIAL SKILLS

Wither skeletons are immune to burning in fire or lava. They may pick up any weapons or armour they find lying on the ground. Like all undead mobs, they are healed by potion of harming, and harmed by potion of healing.

HOW TO DEFEAT

Use the wither skeleton's height against it – get yourself into a 2-block-high space and hit it through the gap with an enchanted diamond sword. You can also stand on a 3-block-high pillar and hit it from above, and throw a splash potion of healing at it.

USEFUL DROPS

Wither skeletons may drop 1 coal, and up to 2 bones which can be crafted into bone meal. Very rarely they will drop their skull – you need 3 wither skeleton skulls to craft the wither boss. See pages 32-33 for more info. They may also drop their sword.

ZOMBIE PIGMAN

HEALTH POINTS	20
ATTACK STRENGTH	5-13
HOW TO DEFEAT	
ITEMS DROPPED	

0-1 0-1 0-1 0-1 5

SPAWN LIGHT LEVEL

15

0

SPAWN LOCATIONS · · · · · ·
Anywhere in the Nether.

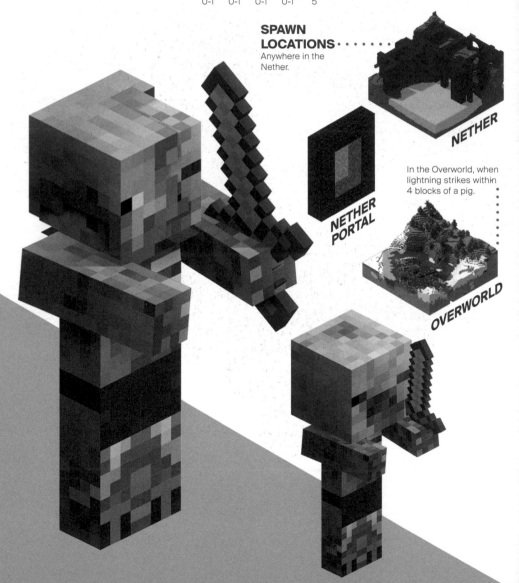

NETHER

NETHER PORTAL

In the Overworld, when lightning strikes within 4 blocks of a pig. · · · ·

OVERWORLD

BEHAVIOUR

Zombie pigmen are the Nether's only neutral mob. When neutral they move slowly and don't do much until they are attacked. The pig-like sounds they make will alert you to their presence.

ATTACK METHOD

Zombie pigmen will leave you alone until you attack, then every pigman in the area will retaliate, hitting you with their swords. Their movement speeds up when aggravated and you can easily find yourself cornered by a large group of them.

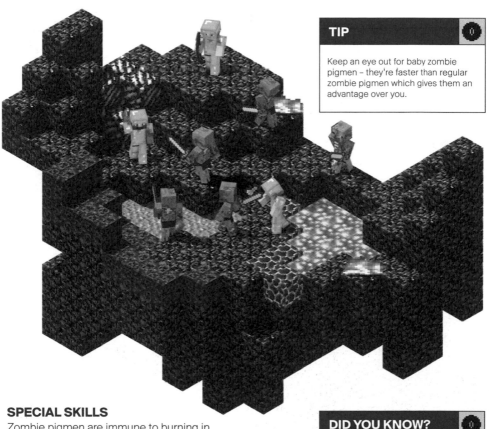

TIP

Keep an eye out for baby zombie pigmen – they're faster than regular zombie pigmen which gives them an advantage over you.

SPECIAL SKILLS

Zombie pigmen are immune to burning in fire and lava. They have the ability to pick up weapons and items. 5% of zombie pigmen will spawn as baby zombie pigmen, and 5% of baby zombie pigmen will be pigman jockeys. Zombie pigmen are immune to poison.

DID YOU KNOW?

Like their Overworld counterparts, zombie pigmen may bang on wooden doors, and can break them down if your difficulty is set to hard.

HOW TO DEFEAT

Pick zombie pigmen off one-by-one to reduce your chances of being swarmed. Shoot them with a bow and arrow from a distance, throw a splash potion of healing at them or stand on a 2-block-high dirt pillar and hit them from above with your sword.

USEFUL DROPS

Zombie pigmen may drop rotten flesh when defeated, which can be used to breed and heal tamed wolves and lead them around. They may also drop a gold nugget or a gold ingot which can be used for crafting, or their golden sword, which may be enchanted.

THE WITHER

HEALTH POINTS	300
ATTACK STRENGTH	5-12
HOW TO DEFEAT	
ITEMS DROPPED	

1   50

**SPAWN
LIGHT
LEVEL**

15

0

TIP

Snow golems are your friend when fighting the wither – they fire snowballs at it and distract the wither from attacking you. Craft a small army of snow golems to increase your chances of success.

SPAWNS · · · · · · · · · · · · · · · · · ·

When crafted by the player, using 4 blocks of soul sand and 3 wither skeleton skulls. The last block placed must be a wither skeleton skull for the wither to spawn.

DID YOU KNOW?

You won't be able to spawn the wither in peaceful mode – the blocks will simply sit there, devoid of life.

TIP

There's a clue to the wither's crafting recipe in one of Minecraft's paintings.

BEHAVIOUR

Once spawned, the wither will flash blue and increase in size as its health bar fills. At this stage the wither is invulnerable and will not move or attack you. At the end of this process the wither creates a very large explosion, which destroys any nearby blocks and mobs. The wither will begin to attack after this explosion. The wither is hostile to players and all mobs except for undead mobs (skeletons, zombies, zombie pigmen, wither skeletons, husks, strays and other withers).

SPECIAL SKILLS

The wither is immune to fire, lava, drowning and suffocation. It also has 300 health points – that's 100 more than the ender dragon.

ATTACK METHOD

Each of its three heads can launch wither skull projectiles so it can attack three players or mobs at the same time. When these skulls make contact with a player they will be inflicted with the wither effect – a health-draining effect that lasts for 40 seconds.

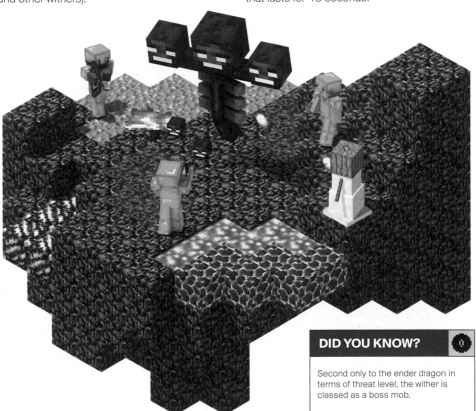

DID YOU KNOW?

Second only to the ender dragon in terms of threat level, the wither is classed as a boss mob.

HOW TO DEFEAT

Move backwards when it begins to flash blue so you don't get caught in the explosion. Once it has exploded, shoot it with an enchanted bow and arrows whilst drinking potions of strength and healing. Like other undead mobs, it's harmed by healing potions so you can throw splash potions of healing at it. You can also hit it with an enchanted diamond sword.

USEFUL DROPS

The wither will drop 1 Nether star if you manage to defeat it. This star will remain on the ground and never despawn until it is picked up. You'll need a Nether star to make a beacon – a useful block that can be placed on top of power pyramids to provide status buffs and a powerful light source. See page 75 for more info.

NETHER FORTRESSES

Nether fortresses are large, naturally generated structures that appear in strips along the z-axis (north-south). They're built from Nether brick and are partially buried in netherrack in several places. They're a great source of materials and loot, if you can negotiate your way past the hostile mobs. Let's take a closer look at the structure.

1 BRIDGES
Several bridges run around the periphery of the fortress. Follow one of these and it will eventually lead you to the interior.

2 BALCONIES
Exterior balconies provide vantage points from which to scan the surrounding area for threats. They're enclosed by Nether brick fence so you won't fall off the edge.

3 LAVA WELL ROOM
These rooms contain nothing except a small lava well – they mark the entry to the inside of the fortress and are found at the end of an exterior bridge.

4 CORRIDORS

Much of the interior of the fortress is made up of corridors. Hostile mobs wander these corridors freely and they are very dimly lit, so be careful when turning corners.

5 LOOT CHEST

Around a third of all Nether fortress corridors contain a loot chest, inside which you might find everything from obsidian to diamond horse armour.

6 NETHER WART STAIRCASES

Nether wart is an important potions ingredient, and it can be found growing at the side of staircases in patches of soul sand.

7 BLAZE SPAWNER PLATFORMS

Blaze spawners sit on raised platforms, accessed by stairs. They regularly produce blazes so you'll want to disable the spawner as quickly as possible.

EXPANDING AND FORTIFYING A NETHER FORTRESS

The existing structure of the Nether fortress can provide a foundation from which to build an impenetrable base, but you'll need to clear out the hostile mobs and make a few fortifications first. Follow these steps to turn it into a secure and intimidating fortress.

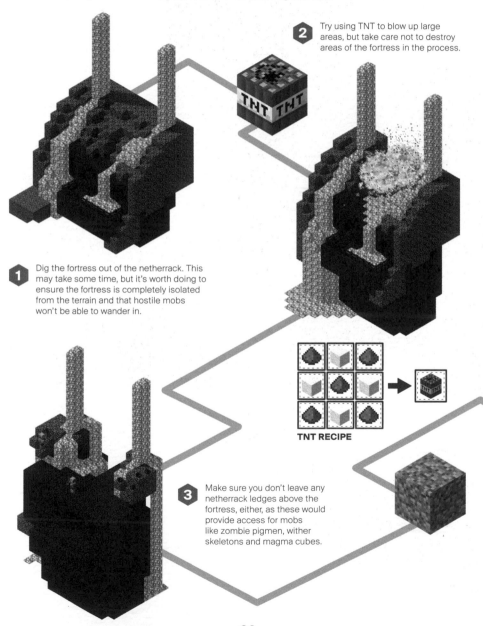

2 Try using TNT to blow up large areas, but take care not to destroy areas of the fortress in the process.

1 Dig the fortress out of the netherrack. This may take some time, but it's worth doing to ensure the fortress is completely isolated from the terrain and that hostile mobs won't be able to wander in.

TNT RECIPE

3 Make sure you don't leave any netherrack ledges above the fortress, either, as these would provide access for mobs like zombie pigmen, wither skeletons and magma cubes.

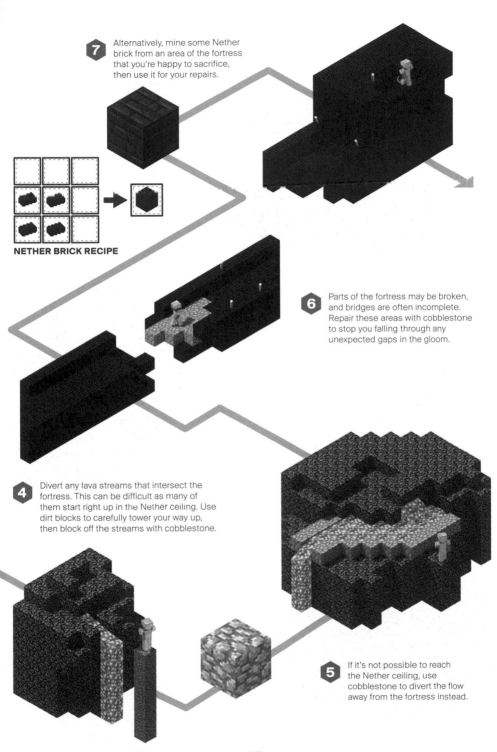

7 Alternatively, mine some Nether brick from an area of the fortress that you're happy to sacrifice, then use it for your repairs.

NETHER BRICK RECIPE

6 Parts of the fortress may be broken, and bridges are often incomplete. Repair these areas with cobblestone to stop you falling through any unexpected gaps in the gloom.

4 Divert any lava streams that intersect the fortress. This can be difficult as many of them start right up in the Nether ceiling. Use dirt blocks to carefully tower your way up, then block off the streams with cobblestone.

5 If it's not possible to reach the Nether ceiling, use cobblestone to divert the flow away from the fortress instead.

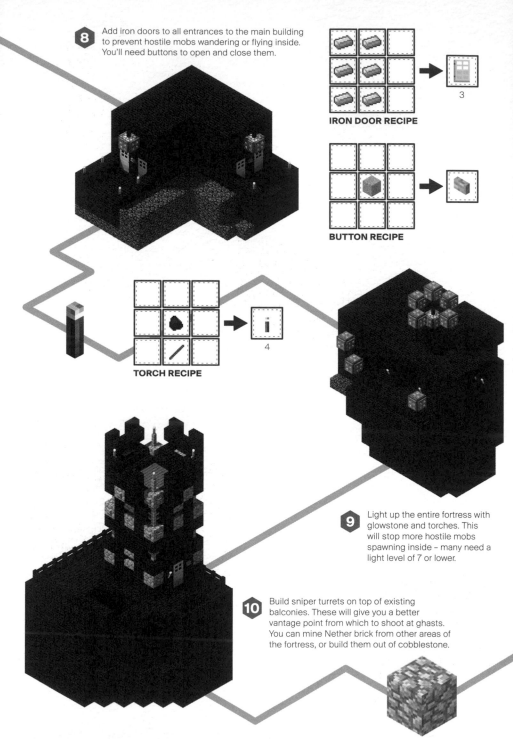

8 Add iron doors to all entrances to the main building to prevent hostile mobs wandering or flying inside. You'll need buttons to open and close them.

IRON DOOR RECIPE

3

BUTTON RECIPE

TORCH RECIPE

4

9 Light up the entire fortress with glowstone and torches. This will stop more hostile mobs spawning inside – many need a light level of 7 or lower.

10 Build sniper turrets on top of existing balconies. These will give you a better vantage point from which to shoot at ghasts. You can mine Nether brick from other areas of the fortress, or build them out of cobblestone.

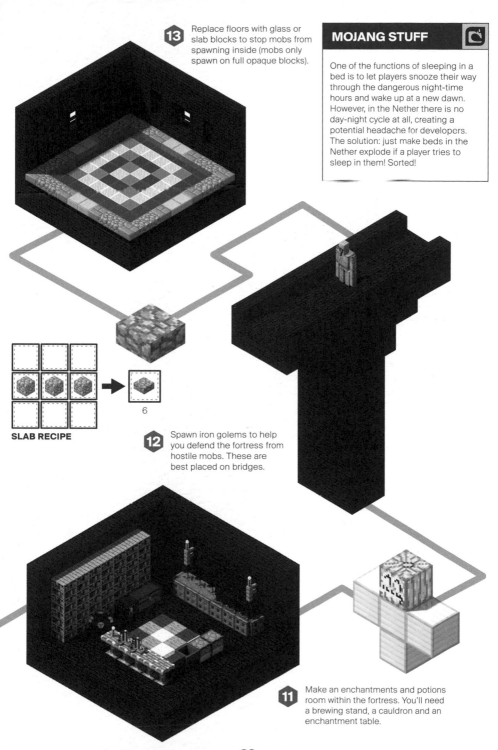

13 Replace floors with glass or slab blocks to stop mobs from spawning inside (mobs only spawn on full opaque blocks).

MOJANG STUFF

One of the functions of sleeping in a bed is to let players snooze their way through the dangerous night-time hours and wake up at a new dawn. However, in the Nether there is no day-night cycle at all, creating a potential headache for developers. The solution: just make beds in the Nether explode if a player tries to sleep in them! Sorted!

SLAB RECIPE

6

12 Spawn iron golems to help you defend the fortress from hostile mobs. These are best placed on bridges.

11 Make an enchantments and potions room within the fortress. You'll need a brewing stand, a cauldron and an enchantment table.

MINECART SYSTEM

An enclosed minecart system will allow you to travel quickly around your fortress and back and forth to your portal, without being swarmed by mobs. Follow these steps to create a fireproof minecart system that can also double up as a fun rollercoaster.

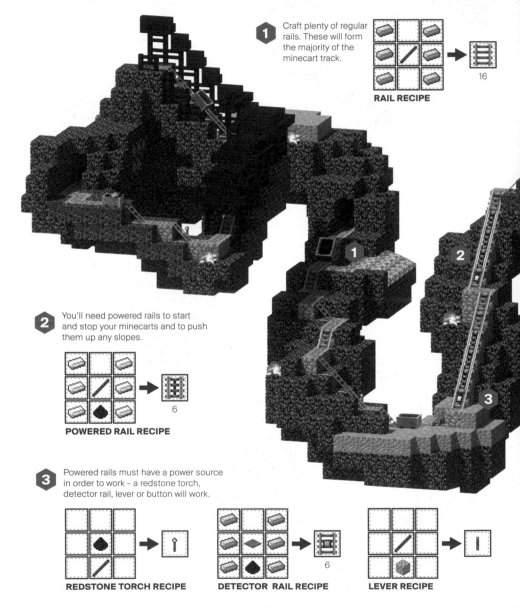

1 Craft plenty of regular rails. These will form the majority of the minecart track.

RAIL RECIPE

16

2 You'll need powered rails to start and stop your minecarts and to push them up any slopes.

6

POWERED RAIL RECIPE

3 Powered rails must have a power source in order to work – a redstone torch, detector rail, lever or button will work.

REDSTONE TORCH RECIPE

DETECTOR RAIL RECIPE

6

LEVER RECIPE

4 Create an outline for your minecart track using cobblestone, then position your rails on top. Place a power source on the block next to each powered rail.

5 Enclose your minecart system in Nether fence and Nether brick blocks, which are immune to fire and lava.

6 Craft a minecart to travel in, then test your system. You may find you need more strategically-placed powered rails.

MINECART RECIPE

FARMING

Mushrooms are the only source of food that grows naturally in the Nether and you can't place water. But that doesn't mean you can't grow your own food – follow these steps to set up a sustainable farm and you'll be able to spend as much time as you like in the Nether without risk of starvation.

TREES
Plant tree saplings to provide you with wood for crafting. You'll just need dirt blocks and a light source. Make sure you leave plenty of space between saplings to ensure that they grow. Oak trees may also drop apples which can be eaten as they are or crafted with gold ingots to make golden apples. Jungle trees can be used to grow cocoa – see page 45.

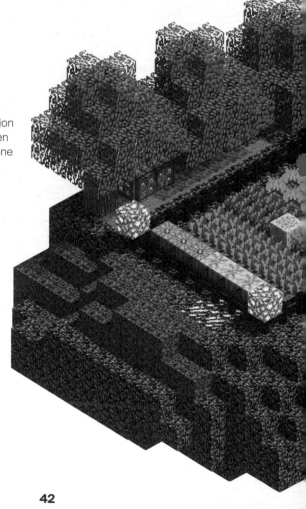

WHEAT, CARROTS, POTATOES AND BEETROOT
Wheat, carrots, potatoes and beetroot will also grow without water – it'll just take longer. Bring dirt across from the Overworld, place it in your desired location then use a hoe to till it into farmland, then plant seeds immediately. Place glowstone blocks along the side to provide light to enable growth.

MELONS AND PUMPKINS
Melons and pumpkins will grow without water – they just need light and an adjacent block to grow into.

DID YOU KNOW?

Wet sponge can be used to provide crops with water in the Nether. Just place blocks next to your farmland to hydrate it. Wet sponge can be found in ocean monuments.

MUSHROOMS

Grow mushrooms on any block. For them to spread there must be fewer than 5 mushrooms in a 9 x 9 x 3 area and the light level in the area must be 12 or lower.

MUSHROOM STEW RECIPE
Mushrooms can be crafted into mushroom stew.

CHICKEN FARMING

Chicken eggs can easily be imported into the Nether. Simply throw them into a pen and approximately 1 in 8 will spawn a chicken. Your pen should be indoors to protect the chickens.

LEADING OTHER ANIMALS INTO THE NETHER

You can lead other animals such as cows, sheep, pigs and horses into the Nether through your portal, but this is tricky, especially if your fortress is some way away from your portal. Consider constructing a new portal at your fortress so you can more easily lead animals across to their new home. The safest way to bring animals across is to attach leads to them first.

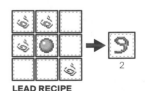

LEAD RECIPE

BAKERY

Importing a few key ingredients from the Overworld will allow you to set up a bakery within your fortress. With cake, bread, cookies and pumpkin pies available your chances of survival just got a lot higher!

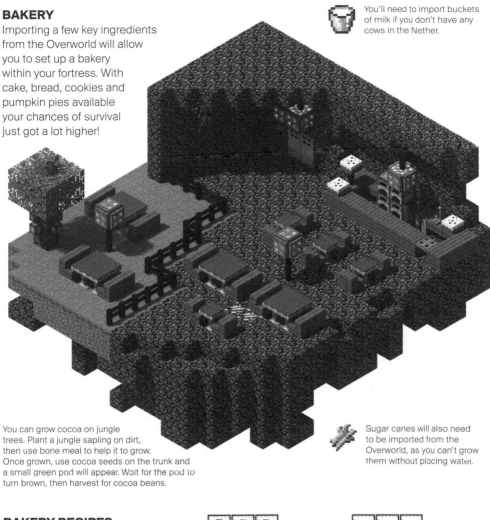

You'll need to import buckets of milk if you don't have any cows in the Nether.

You can grow cocoa on jungle trees. Plant a jungle sapling on dirt, then use bone meal to help it to grow. Once grown, use cocoa seeds on the trunk and a small green pod will appear. Wait for the pod to turn brown, then harvest for cocoa beans.

Sugar canes will also need to be imported from the Overworld, as you can't grow them without placing water.

BAKERY RECIPES

Once you've collected all these ingredients you can craft the items shown to the right, which will restore higher levels of food points.

CAKE RECIPE

PUMPKIN PIE RECIPE

BREAD RECIPE

COOKIE RECIPE

8

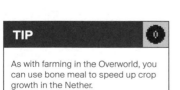

TIP

As with farming in the Overworld, you can use bone meal to speed up crop growth in the Nether.

2

THE END

Now that you've conquered the Nether you can brew potions and prepare for the ultimate challenge. In this section you'll learn how to get to the dangerous End dimension, what to do when faced with the ultimate boss mob – the ender dragon – and where to look for the rarest blocks and items if you manage to defeat it.

THE END ENVIRONMENT

The End is a cluster of islands surrounded by a vast nothingness known simply as The Void. There is no day or night, just perpetual darkness. For many players it's the ultimate adventure: with barely any resources and Minecraft's boss mob, the ender dragon, living there, it's the ultimate survival challenge.

 1 All the islands are composed of End stone. This substance has a higher blast resistance than regular stone and can be mined with a pickaxe.

 2 The main island in the centre is home to the ender dragon. There's not much there, except for a small podium and several obsidian pillars with ender crystals on top, some of which are protected by iron bars. The obsidian and iron bars can be mined once you've defeated the dragon, but you'll need to destroy the crystals. See pages 56-59 for more info.

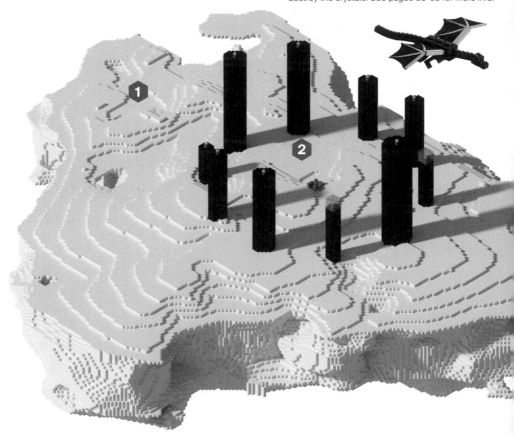

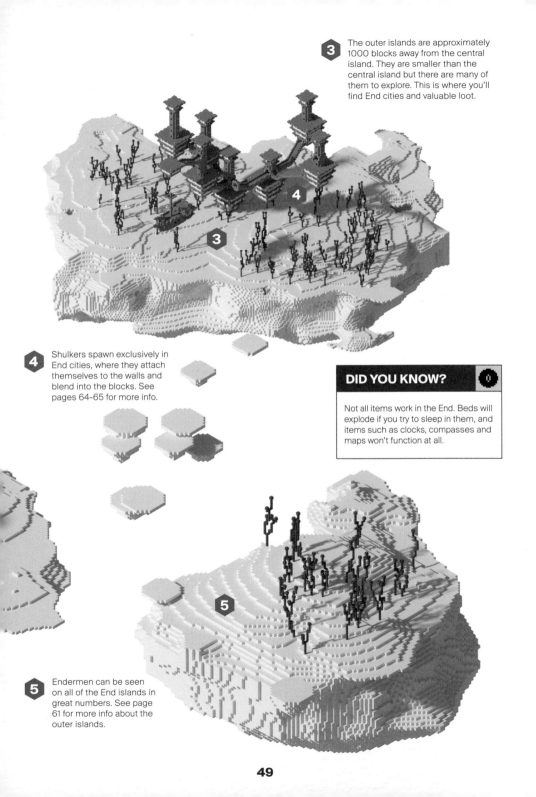

3 The outer islands are approximately 1000 blocks away from the central island. They are smaller than the central island but there are many of them to explore. This is where you'll find End cities and valuable loot.

4 Shulkers spawn exclusively in End cities, where they attach themselves to the walls and blend into the blocks. See pages 64-65 for more info.

DID YOU KNOW? **0**

Not all items work in the End. Beds will explode if you try to sleep in them, and items such as clocks, compasses and maps won't function at all.

5 Endermen can be seen on all of the End islands in great numbers. See page 61 for more info about the outer islands.

PREPARING FOR A TRIP TO THE END

Given the danger that awaits, you must take special care to prepare for a trip to the End. It's not just the ender dragon you need to worry about, there are also endermen and shulkers, and the danger of falling into the Void. Let's look at what you'll need to take with you if you hope to survive.

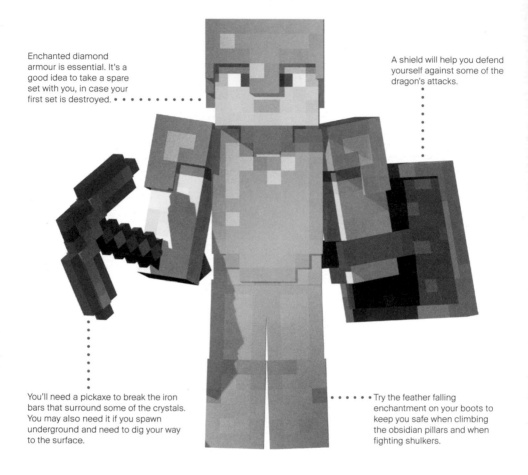

Enchanted diamond armour is essential. It's a good idea to take a spare set with you, in case your first set is destroyed.

A shield will help you defend yourself against some of the dragon's attacks.

You'll need a pickaxe to break the iron bars that surround some of the crystals. You may also need it if you spawn underground and need to dig your way to the surface.

Try the feather falling enchantment on your boots to keep you safe when climbing the obsidian pillars and when fighting shulkers.

 A pumpkin can be worn instead of a helmet to stop endermen becoming hostile if you look directly at them. Just be aware it won't provide any protection.

 Eyes of ender are necessary to locate a stronghold and repair the End portal. See pages 52-53.

 You'll need an enchanted bow and arrows of harming to deal damage to the ender dragon.

 You may spawn on a platform a short distance away from the main island, so you'll need ender pearls to teleport. You'll also need them once you've defeated the dragon.

 An enchanted diamond sword is the best choice of weapon for close-combat with the dragon.

 Take several stacks of good-quality food such as steak and cake to keep your food and health bars topped up.

You'll need glass bottles to collect dragon's breath. See page 56-57 for more about this valuable substance.

Take an emergency stack of obsidian to make a panic shelter.

You'll need potions of healing, swiftness and strength to restore your health, as well as splash potions of harming to throw at the dragon.

A stack of dirt blocks will come in handy for towering your way up the obsidian pillars to reach the crystals.

Endermen take damage from water, so take several water buckets in case you need to defend yourself.

You'll need at least 12 beds – see page 59 for more info on how these are helpful.

LOCATING A STRONGHOLD

A stronghold is a naturally generated structure that contains a gateway to the End dimension. There are only a limited number per world (128) and they're hidden underground. Follow these steps to locate your nearest stronghold.

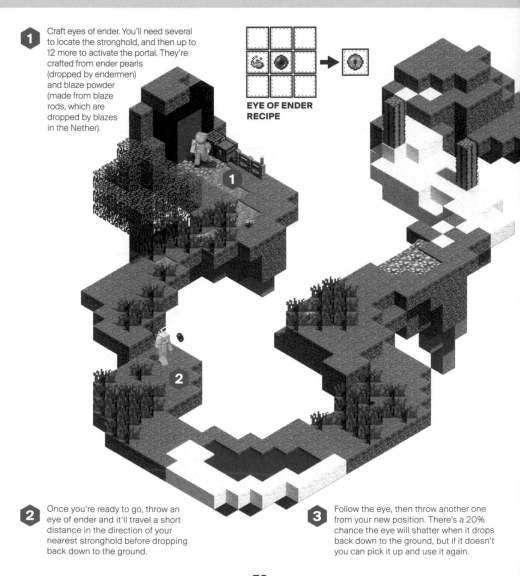

1 Craft eyes of ender. You'll need several to locate the stronghold, and then up to 12 more to activate the portal. They're crafted from ender pearls (dropped by endermen) and blaze powder (made from blaze rods, which are dropped by blazes in the Nether).

EYE OF ENDER RECIPE

2 Once you're ready to go, throw an eye of ender and it'll travel a short distance in the direction of your nearest stronghold before dropping back down to the ground.

3 Follow the eye, then throw another one from your new position. There's a 20% chance the eye will shatter when it drops back down to the ground, but if it doesn't you can pick it up and use it again.

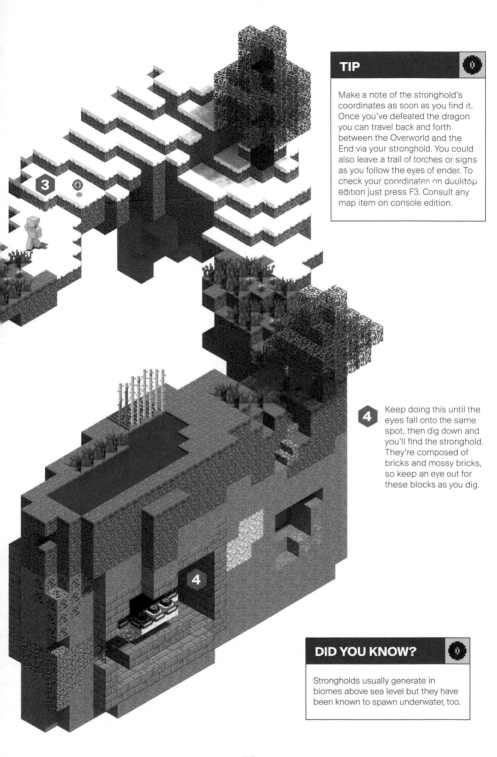

TIP

Make a note of the stronghold's coordinates as soon as you find it. Once you've defeated the dragon you can travel back and forth between the Overworld and the End via your stronghold. You could also leave a trail of torches or signs as you follow the eyes of ender. To check your coordinates on desktop edition just press F3. Consult any map item on console edition.

4 Keep doing this until the eyes fall onto the same spot, then dig down and you'll find the stronghold. They're composed of bricks and mossy bricks, so keep an eye out for these blocks as you dig.

DID YOU KNOW?

Strongholds usually generate in biomes above sea level but they have been known to spawn underwater, too.

NAVIGATING THE STRONGHOLD

Strongholds are sprawling structures with several rooms linked by corridors and stairs. Each stronghold has a unique layout, and they vary in size, but they always contain an End portal room. As its name suggests, this room is where you'll find the portal that will transport you to the End.

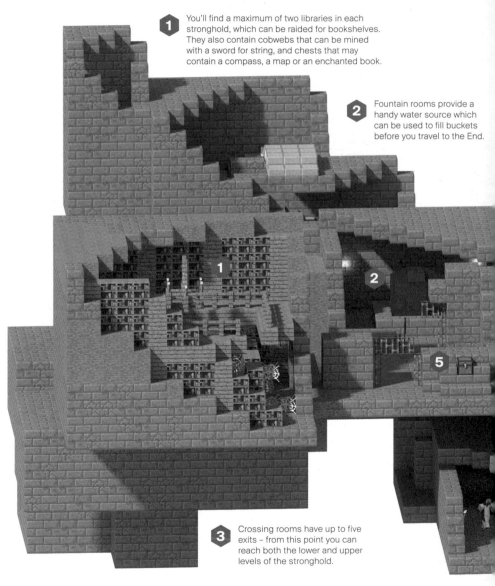

1 You'll find a maximum of two libraries in each stronghold, which can be raided for bookshelves. They also contain cobwebs that can be mined with a sword for string, and chests that may contain a compass, a map or an enchanted book.

2 Fountain rooms provide a handy water source which can be used to fill buckets before you travel to the End.

3 Crossing rooms have up to five exits – from this point you can reach both the lower and upper levels of the stronghold.

4 There are many empty prison cells which can be raided for iron bars and buttons.

5 Some of the stronghold corridors contain loot chests. You can find some very useful items inside, including ender pearls, diamonds and horse armour.

TIP

The portal will deposit you either on, or near, the End's main island so you'll need to be prepared for immediate combat.

6 The End portal room usually contains an incomplete portal, except for rare cases where all 12 portal frames contain eyes of ender. It also contains a silverfish spawner and two lava pools. To activate an incomplete portal you'll need to place eyes of ender in the empty frames, then jump through.

7 There's a realistic chance that the ender dragon will defeat you, so you should be prepared to respawn. Before you enter the End for the first time, place a chest full of backup supplies in the portal room so that you can quickly return for round two. Make sure it includes a full set of armour, a pumpkin, weapons, potions, food and ender pearls.

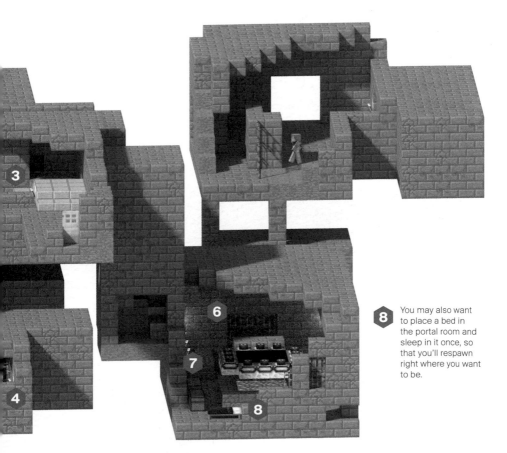

8 You may also want to place a bed in the portal room and sleep in it once, so that you'll respawn right where you want to be.

THE ENDER DRAGON

The ender dragon is Minecraft's deadliest boss mob. With an intimidating number of health points and some devastating attack methods, defeating it is no easy task. Let's take a look at what you're dealing with.

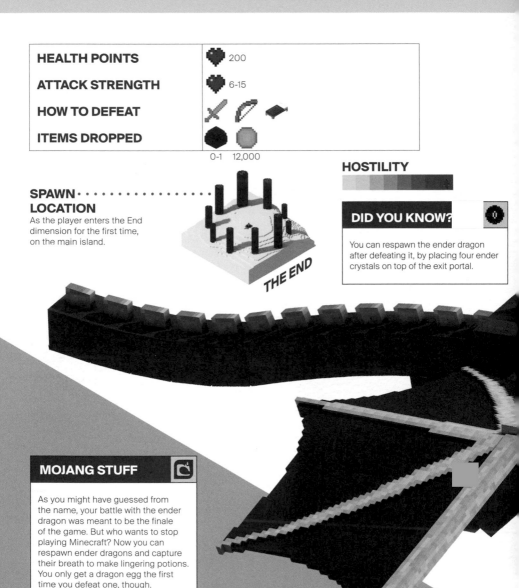

HEALTH POINTS	200	
ATTACK STRENGTH	6-15	
HOW TO DEFEAT		
ITEMS DROPPED	0-1 12,000	

HOSTILITY

SPAWN LOCATION

As the player enters the End dimension for the first time, on the main island.

THE END

DID YOU KNOW?

You can respawn the ender dragon after defeating it, by placing four ender crystals on top of the exit portal.

MOJANG STUFF

As you might have guessed from the name, your battle with the ender dragon was meant to be the finale of the game. But who wants to stop playing Minecraft? Now you can respawn ender dragons and capture their breath to make lingering potions. You only get a dragon egg the first time you defeat one, though.

BEHAVIOUR

The ender dragon spends its life circling the main island. It seems to be protective of the podium in the centre, and when not attacking the player it flies down and perches on this podium.

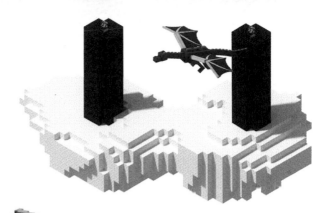

SPECIAL SKILLS

In addition to its enormous size and high number of health points, the dragon has the ability to recharge its health by drawing power from the crystals on top of each obsidian pillar on the main island.

ATTACK METHOD

The dragon will charge, attacking its target with its breath and with ender charges – fireballs that emit harmful purple clouds on contact.

FIGHTING THE DRAGON

Once you step foot in the End there's no way out unless you defeat the ender dragon, or die trying. And defeating the dragon is arguably the most difficult thing you'll ever do in Minecraft, so you must be prepared. These combat tips will give you the best chance of success.

DID YOU KNOW?

You won't always spawn right on the main island – sometimes you'll be on a nearby platform and will need to teleport or build your way across.

MOJANG STUFF

Originally introduced for the 1.0 release of the game on PC, the fight was modified for its console version. But the PC devs liked so many of the changes that they then adopted them on PC, also introducing new phases to the battle, adding cages to the ender crystals and making it harder. Too hard, in fact – many of the developers themselves struggled to complete it, and the difficulty had to be scaled back again!

1 As soon as you arrive in the End, drink a potion of regeneration. Take a moment to look around for the dragon, but don't underestimate the endermen's ability to seriously ruin your day. Consider wearing a pumpkin instead of a helmet so they don't become hostile if you look at them.

2 The dragon draws power from the crystals on top of the obsidian pillars, so you'll need to destroy these before attempting to slay the dragon. Start with the crystals that aren't encased in iron bars – you can shoot them from the ground with arrows.

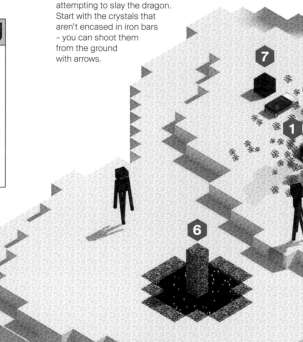

3 You'll need to climb up the obsidian pillars to destroy the crystals encased in iron bars. Use dirt blocks to tower your way to the top, or use ender pearls to teleport then quickly place blocks below your feet. Break the iron bars with your pickaxe and destroy the crystal with your enchanted diamond sword.

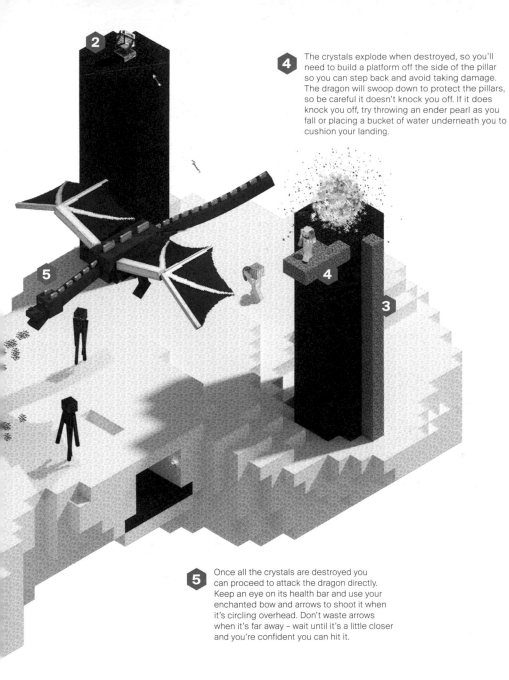

The crystals explode when destroyed, so you'll need to build a platform off the side of the pillar so you can step back and avoid taking damage. The dragon will swoop down to protect the pillars, so be careful it doesn't knock you off. If it does knock you off, try throwing an ender pearl as you fall or placing a bucket of water underneath you to cushion your landing.

Once all the crystals are destroyed you can proceed to attack the dragon directly. Keep an eye on its health bar and use your enchanted bow and arrows to shoot it when it's circling overhead. Don't waste arrows when it's far away – wait until it's a little closer and you're confident you can hit it.

The dragon will swoop down to land on the podium in the centre of the island every few seconds. It's immune to arrows when on the podium, but use your sword to hit its head, or throw a splash potion of harming at it.

To finish it off, place a bed on the ground in front of you, then try to sleep in it when it gets close enough. If you place a block of obsidian between yourself and the bed, it will protect you from some of the blast. You'll need to do this several times to defeat the dragon.

VICTORY

Victory is sweet! Once the dragon's health bar reaches zero it will explode, dropping an incredible 12,000 experience points. You'll also be rewarded with the highly coveted dragon egg which will appear on top of the exit portal which has materialised as if by magic in the centre of the island.

COLLECTING THE EGG

There's a catch: if you try to mine the egg it will unhelpfully teleport away.

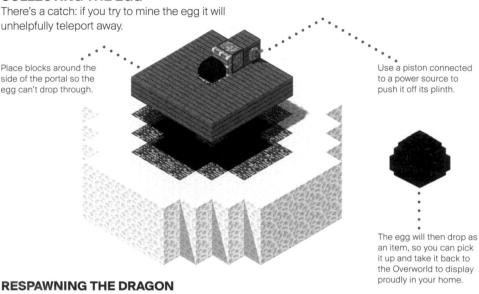

Place blocks around the side of the portal so the egg can't drop through.

Use a piston connected to a power source to push it off its plinth.

The egg will then drop as an item, so you can pick it up and take it back to the Overworld to display proudly in your home.

RESPAWNING THE DRAGON

Keen to stock up on dragon's breath for lingering potions? Then you'll need to respawn the dragon.

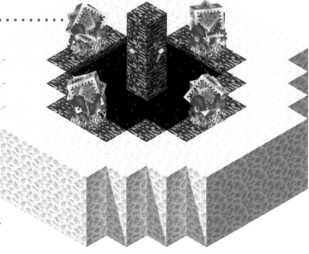

You'll need to place 4 ender crystals around the exit portal – one on each side. An ender crystal can be crafted from an eye of ender, a ghast tear and 7 glass blocks.

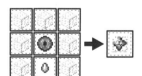

ENDER CRYSTAL RECIPE

Once the final crystal is placed it will regenerate the crystals on top of the pillars, and the dragon will appear. Be warned: if you respawn the dragon you won't be able to leave the End again until it is defeated.

WHERE NEXT?

Two portals appear when you defeat the dragon. The exit portal in the centre of the island will take you back to the Overworld, and a gateway portal will appear at the edge of the island – this leads to another gateway portal on the outer islands. If you choose the exit portal the End Poem will reveal itself to you before you arrive back in the Overworld. This intriguing text is worth a read.

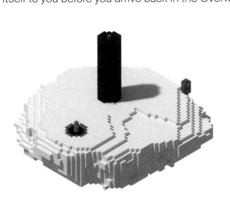 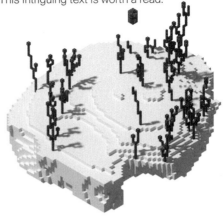

THE OUTER ISLANDS

The outer islands are approximately 1000 blocks away from the main island. As you'll see, the gateway portal that leads to the outer islands is only one block in size. To get through to the other side you'll need to throw an ender pearl into the portal and teleport across. The portal will transport you to one of the nearest outer islands, and from there you can explore the rest of the islands.

There are several useful materials to collect, but there are also endermen and shulkers to deal with. And it's easy to get lost as everything looks very similar.

You'll need to find a way to bridge the gaps between the outer islands so you don't fall into the Void. If you have enough cobblestone you can build cobblestone bridges between the islands so you can travel around safely.

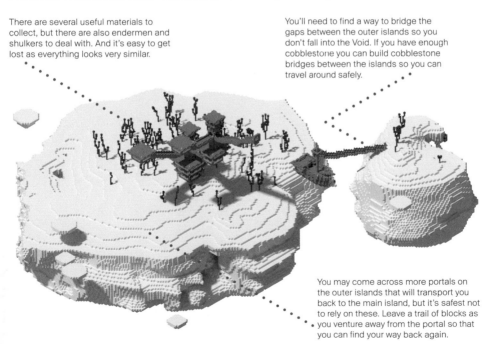

You may come across more portals on the outer islands that will transport you back to the main island, but it's safest not to rely on these. Leave a trail of blocks as you venture away from the portal so that you can find your way back again.

END CITIES

End cities are mysterious naturally generated structures found on the outer islands. They aren't a common sight so it can take a while to locate one. Let's take a look at the structures you'll find in End cities.

STRUCTURES

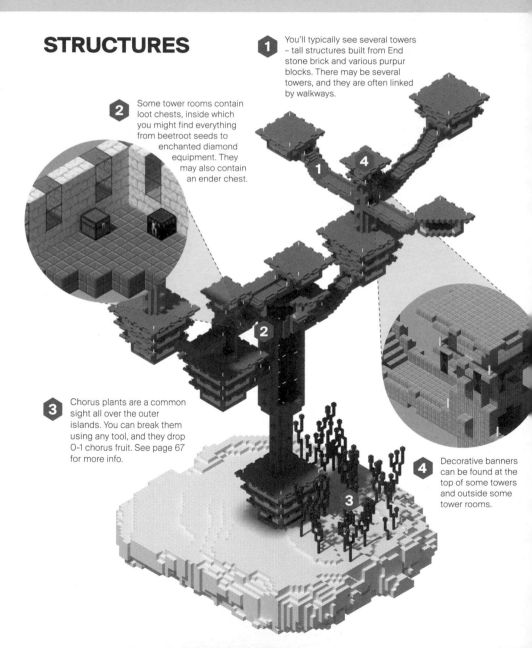

1 You'll typically see several towers – tall structures built from End stone brick and various purpur blocks. There may be several towers, and they are often linked by walkways.

2 Some tower rooms contain loot chests, inside which you might find everything from beetroot seeds to enchanted diamond equipment. They may also contain an ender chest.

3 Chorus plants are a common sight all over the outer islands. You can break them using any tool, and they drop 0-1 chorus fruit. See page 67 for more info.

4 Decorative banners can be found at the top of some towers and outside some tower rooms.

TIP

End ships may be found at the end of piers in End cities. The easiest way to reach these floating ships is to walk to the end of the pier and throw an ender pearl to teleport across the gap.

5 There's a brewing room inside the ship, where you'll find a brewing stand and two potions of healing that may come in useful if you've taken a lot of damage. A staircase leads from the brewing room to the treasure room below.

6 End rods can be found all over End cities, and provide the only source of light on the outer islands. They can be mined with any tool. You'll also find a dragon head on the bow of the ship – the only place that this rare item generates.

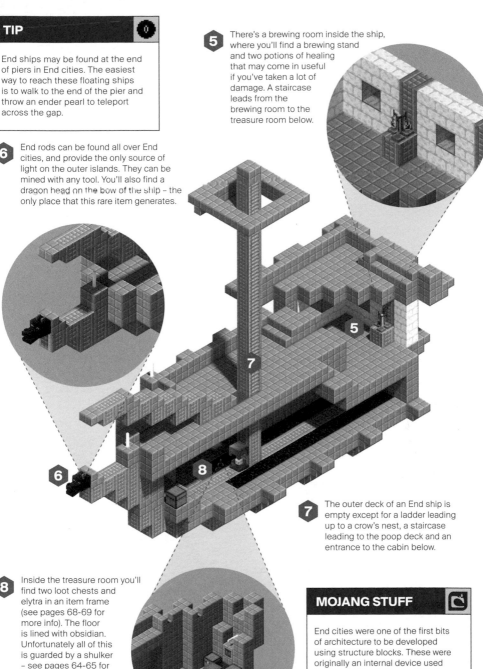

7 The outer deck of an End ship is empty except for a ladder leading up to a crow's nest, a staircase leading to the poop deck and an entrance to the cabin below.

8 Inside the treasure room you'll find two loot chests and elytra in an item frame (see pages 68-69 for more info). The floor is lined with obsidian. Unfortunately all of this is guarded by a shulker – see pages 64-65 for tips on how to deal with these creatures.

MOJANG STUFF

End cities were one of the first bits of architecture to be developed using structure blocks. These were originally an internal device used to save and load structures, but they were so useful that they were released to the community as a creative tool.

SHULKER

HEALTH POINTS	💜 30
ATTACK STRENGTH	💜 4
HOW TO DEFEAT	
ITEMS DROPPED	0-1 5

SPAWN LIGHT LEVEL

MOJANG STUFF

The initial plans were to create a constructable, golem-like mob for End Cities, but the design just never came together in a fun way. Then, in a flash of inspiration, Jens had the idea of a mob that lived inside blocks!

SPAWN LOCATION

In End cities attached to solid blocks, usually on the walls.

END CITY

BEHAVIOUR

Shulkers attach themselves to solid blocks. They generally lie dormant with their shell closed to blend in with the purpur blocks. Every so often they open their shell a little way to look for targets, revealing a vulnerable, fleshy creature inside.

ATTACK METHOD

When a shulker detects a target within 16 blocks they open their shell and shoot a projectile which follows the target and deals 4 health points of damage upon contact. It also administers the levitation effect for 10 seconds – when the effect wears off they fall back down to the ground, taking damage.

SPECIAL SKILLS

Shulkers camouflage themselves into the purpur blocks. They're immune to lava and fire and, when their shell is closed, they're immune to arrows. When one shulker is attacked any shulkers in the area will retaliate. When their health drops to less than half a heart they will teleport away to protect themselves.

SHULKER BOX RECIPE

HOW TO DEFEAT

Wait until the shulker opens its shell, then hit the creature inside with your enchanted diamond sword. You can also attempt to deflect the shulker's projectiles with a sword, a bow and arrow or your hands, or block them with your shield.

USEFUL DROPS

Shulkers may drop their shell when defeated, which can then be crafted with a chest to make a shulker box. These clever blocks have 27 storage slots and can store and transport items, and will even keep their items when broken with a pickaxe.

END BLOCKS & ITEMS & THEIR USES

Once you've dealt with the endermen and shulkers you can help yourself to the End city's unique blocks and items. Take a look at what you can do with these materials back in the Overworld.

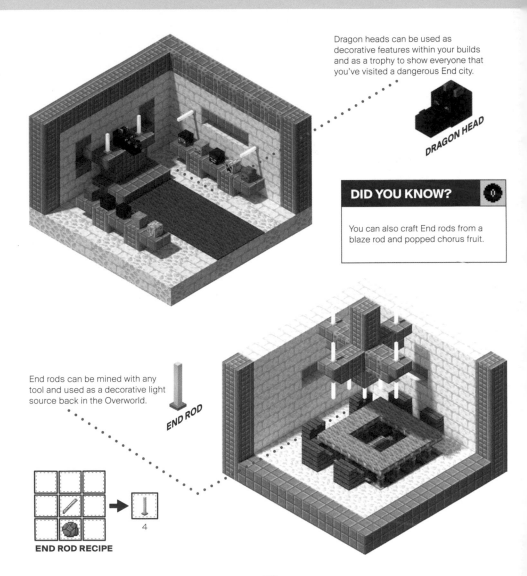

Dragon heads can be used as decorative features within your builds and as a trophy to show everyone that you've visited a dangerous End city.

DRAGON HEAD

DID YOU KNOW?

You can also craft End rods from a blaze rod and popped chorus fruit.

End rods can be mined with any tool and used as a decorative light source back in the Overworld.

END ROD

4

END ROD RECIPE

CHORUS FRUIT
Restores 4 food points

POPPED CHORUS FRUIT

Chorus fruit can be eaten, or cooked in a furnace to produce popped chorus fruit which can be used to craft purpur blocks and End rods.

END STONE BRICKS RECIPE

Purpur blocks have a blast resistance of 30 and can be used for construction back in the Overworld. They can also be crafted into stairs, slabs and pillars to add detail to your builds

PURPUR STAIRS

PURPUR PILLAR

PURPUR SLAB

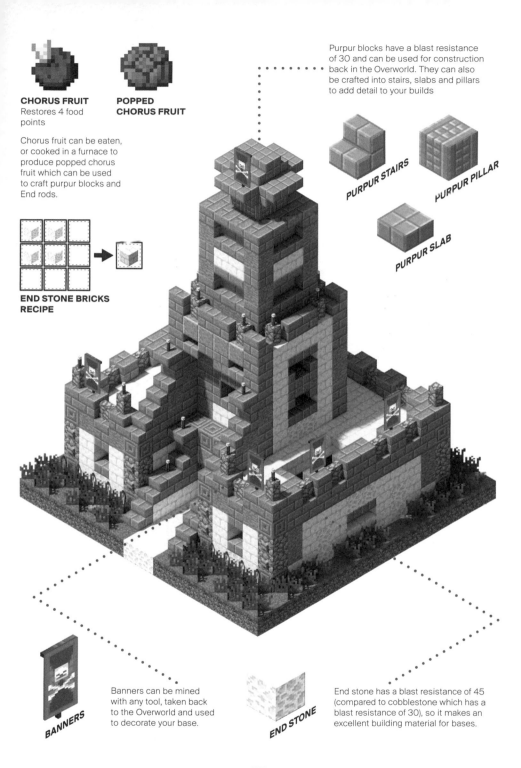

BANNERS

Banners can be mined with any tool, taken back to the Overworld and used to decorate your base.

END STONE

End stone has a blast resistance of 45 (compared to cobblestone which has a blast resistance of 30), so it makes an excellent building material for bases.

ELYTRA

Elytra are wearable wings that allow you to glide through the air. Their default appearance is grey, but if you're wearing a cape they will cleverly adopt the cape's design. These wings are the closest you'll come to flying in Survival mode, so make sure you pick some up from your local End city.

HOW TO USE

Equip the elytra in your chestplate slot. When you're ready, jump from a height, e.g. off a cliff or building. Jump again when in mid-air to activate them. Once you're gliding, simply look left or right to change direction. Look up and down to change your speed and how quickly you descend.

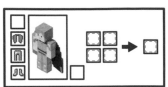

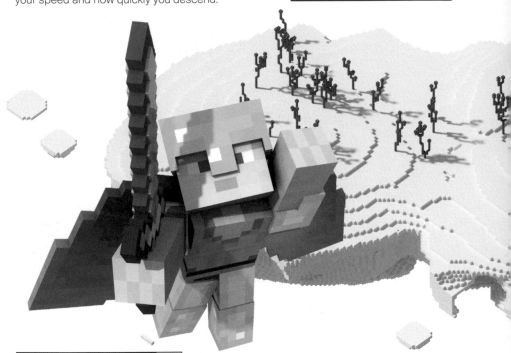

MOJANG STUFF

Elytra need to be activated after a jump or a fall, but this wasn't always the case. Back then you could also attach elytra to mobs, teleport them into the air and watch them swoop about – but by making the elytra activation-only, mobs just dropped like rocks. This would never do! By popular demand, elytra now automatically activate when attached to mobs.

DURABILITY

Elytra have a durability of 431, and this decreases by one point for each second they're in use. So, one pair of elytra will give you 7 minutes and 11 seconds of flight. When their durability reaches 1 they stop working.

REPAIR

Fortunately you can repair them – you can craft two damaged elytra together on an anvil or one elytra with leather. Each piece of leather repairs 108 durability points, so you'll need 4 pieces of leather to restore them to full durability.

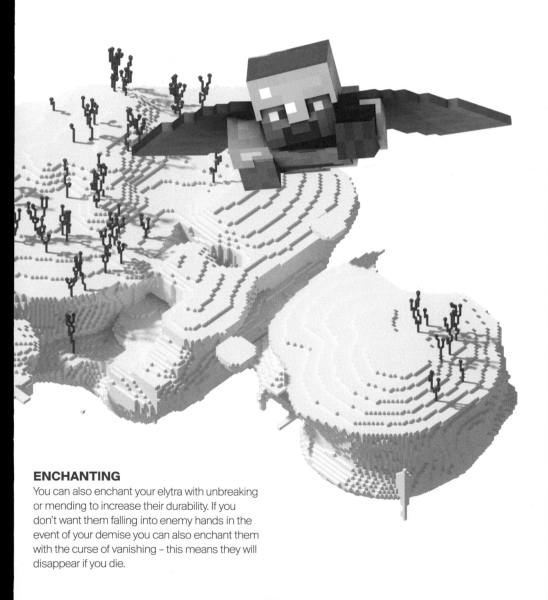

ENCHANTING

You can also enchant your elytra with unbreaking or mending to increase their durability. If you don't want them falling into enemy hands in the event of your demise you can also enchant them with the curse of vanishing – this means they will disappear if you die.

SETTLING IN THE END

Now that you've conquered the End you can make it into a permanent base of operations. Thanks to return portals (portals found near End cities that transport you back to the main island) you'll be able to travel back and forth between the islands, and back to the Overworld via your stronghold to import supplies.

MAIN ISLAND

Let's take a look at how you can develop the main island into a more permanent settlement.

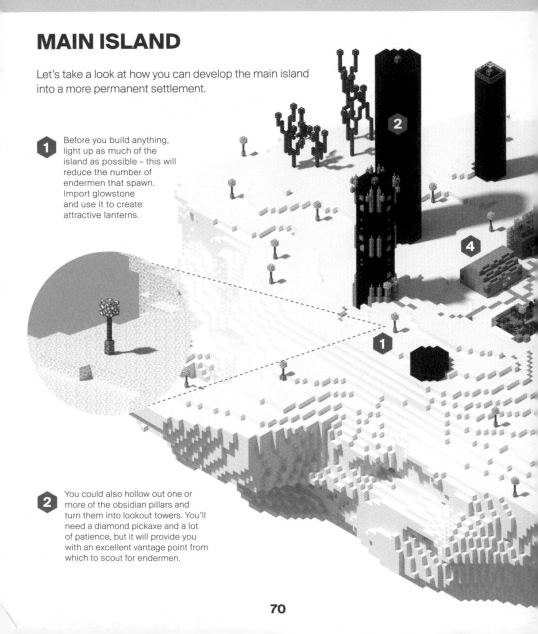

1 Before you build anything, light up as much of the island as possible – this will reduce the number of endermen that spawn. Import glowstone and use it to create attractive lanterns.

2 You could also hollow out one or more of the obsidian pillars and turn them into lookout towers. You'll need a diamond pickaxe and a lot of patience, but it will provide you with an excellent vantage point from which to scout for endermen.

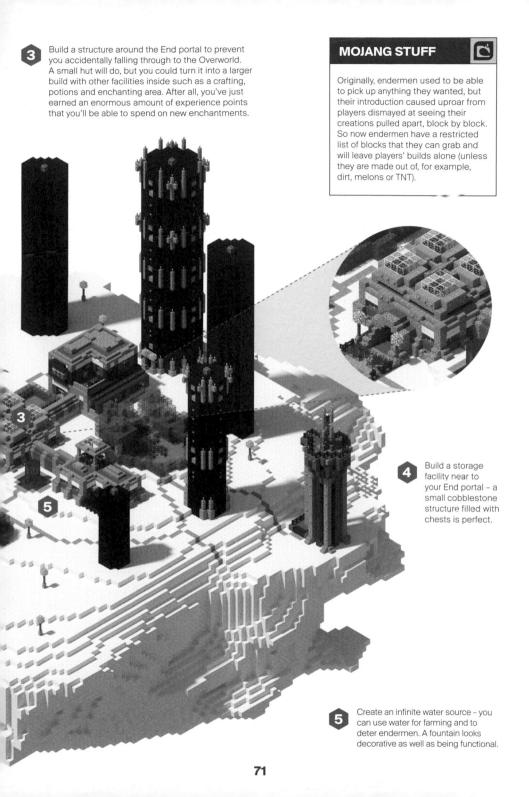

3 Build a structure around the End portal to prevent you accidentally falling through to the Overworld. A small hut will do, but you could turn it into a larger build with other facilities inside such as a crafting, potions and enchanting area. After all, you've just earned an enormous amount of experience points that you'll be able to spend on new enchantments.

MOJANG STUFF

Originally, endermen used to be able to pick up anything they wanted, but their introduction caused uproar from players dismayed at seeing their creations pulled apart, block by block. So now endermen have a restricted list of blocks that they can grab and will leave players' builds alone (unless they are made out of, for example, dirt, melons or TNT).

4 Build a storage facility near to your End portal – a small cobblestone structure filled with chests is perfect.

5 Create an infinite water source – you can use water for farming and to deter endermen. A fountain looks decorative as well as being functional.

71

OUTER ISLANDS

It makes sense to take advantage of the End's existing structures by expanding an End city settlement on one of the outer islands. There's plenty of flat, empty space around these cities, as well as an abundance of End stone that you can use for construction.

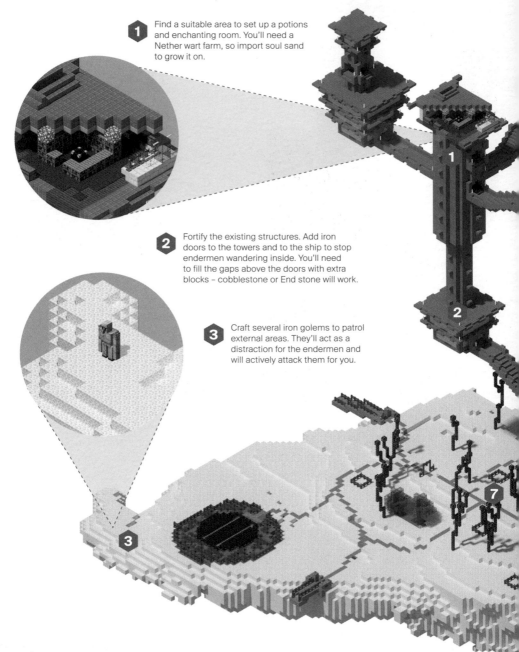

1 Find a suitable area to set up a potions and enchanting room. You'll need a Nether wart farm, so import soul sand to grow it on.

2 Fortify the existing structures. Add iron doors to the towers and to the ship to stop endermen wandering inside. You'll need to fill the gaps above the doors with extra blocks – cobblestone or End stone will work.

3 Craft several iron golems to patrol external areas. They'll act as a distraction for the endermen and will actively attack them for you.

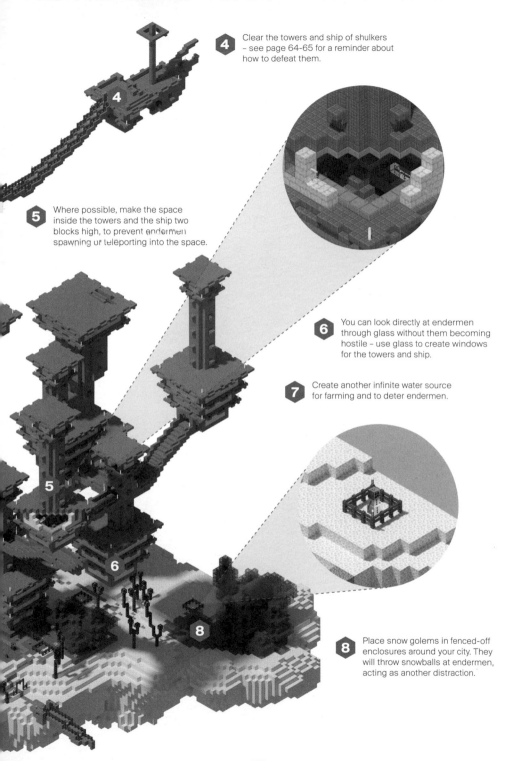

4 Clear the towers and ship of shulkers – see page 64-65 for a reminder about how to defeat them.

5 Where possible, make the space inside the towers and the ship two blocks high, to prevent endermen spawning or teleporting into the space.

6 You can look directly at endermen through glass without them becoming hostile – use glass to create windows for the towers and ship.

7 Create another infinite water source for farming and to deter endermen.

8 Place snow golems in fenced-off enclosures around your city. They will throw snowballs at endermen, acting as another distraction.

OUTER ISLANDS

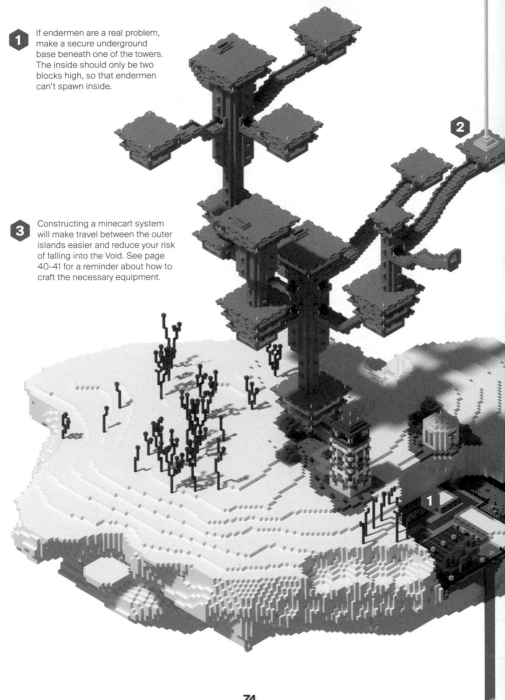

1 If endermen are a real problem, make a secure underground base beneath one of the towers. The inside should only be two blocks high, so that endermen can't spawn inside.

3 Constructing a minecart system will make travel between the outer islands easier and reduce your risk of falling into the Void. See page 40-41 for a reminder about how to craft the necessary equipment.

2 If you have the necessary resources you can build a power pyramid near the city and place a beacon block on top of it. This structure will provide you with special buffs when you're within a certain range. When placed, the beacon block will need an unobstructed view of the sky, and it must be on top of a pyramid, made of solid diamond, emerald, gold or iron blocks.

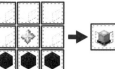

BEACON RECIPE

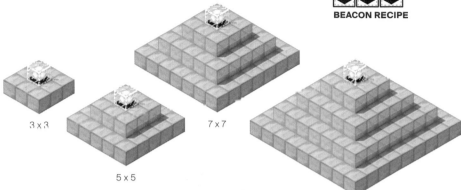

3 x 3

7 x 7

5 x 5

9 x 9

DID YOU KNOW?

There are four levels of pyramid: a level 1 pyramid is 3 x 3 blocks. To make a level 2 pyramid you can add a 5 x 5 base. A level 3 pyramid requires an additional 7 x 7 base and a level 4 pyramid requires an additional 9 x 9 base.

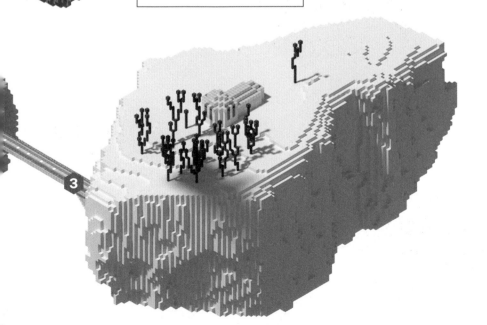

RESOURCES

If you'll be spending a significant amount of time in the End you'll need a supply of resources like food, wood and cobblestone. You can grow crops and breed chickens in the End and, unlike the Nether, you have the added bonus of being able to place water. Let's take a look at the resources you can produce.

WHEAT, BEETROOT, CARROTS AND POTATOES

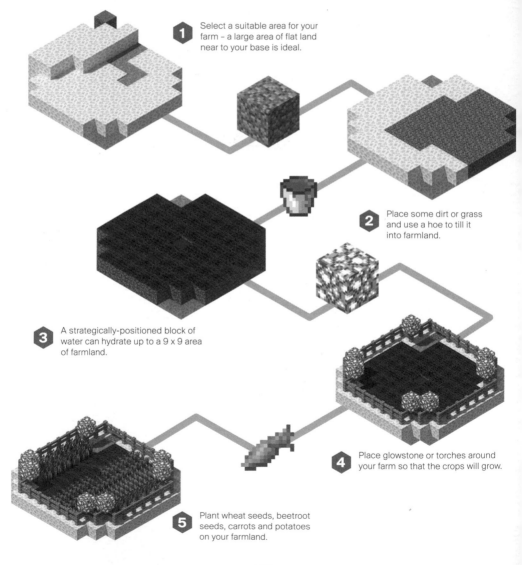

1 Select a suitable area for your farm – a large area of flat land near to your base is ideal.

2 Place some dirt or grass and use a hoe to till it into farmland.

3 A strategically-positioned block of water can hydrate up to a 9 x 9 area of farmland.

4 Place glowstone or torches around your farm so that the crops will grow.

5 Plant wheat seeds, beetroot seeds, carrots and potatoes on your farmland.

SUGAR CANES

Sugar canes can grow on grass, dirt or sand, as long as there's a water source on one side.

MELONS AND PUMPKINS

Melons and pumpkins just need farmland, light and an adjacent block to grow into.

TREE FARM

Cover a large area with dirt blocks and plant saplings 2 blocks apart. They need a light level of 8 or higher to grow, so place torches or glowstone lamps around your farm. Oak trees also provide you with apples if you destroy the leaves, and if you plant jungle tree saplings you can grow cocoa on their trunks.

TIP

Although it is possible to push mobs like cows and pigs through the End portal to get them into the End, it can be tricky. Instead, craft ender chests and set one up in the Overworld and one in the End city. Then you can place meat and other useful animal drops in the Overworld chest and access them in the End.

COBBLESTONE GENERATOR

Cobblestone is useful for building structures and for creating tools and weapons. It doesn't generate naturally in the End, but is created when a lava stream comes into contact with water. Create a ten-block long trench then place a water source block at one end and a lava source block at the other to make a cobblestone generator.

FLOWERS

The End is a barren, inhospitable place, so anything you can do to brighten it up will make you feel more at home. Import some colourful flowers from the Overworld and plant them around the city.

FINAL WORDS

Congratulations, 'crafter. With the knowledge contained in this book, you can be sure to face the terrors of the Nether and the End with confidence. Not too much confidence, mind you: these places are still among the most deadly Minecraft has to offer. Even the strongest, wisest warrior can come unstuck and take a tumble into a pond of molten rock. But you're as well equipped as you can be to overcome such peril, claim the great riches of these strange lands and journey on, finding new adventure. You may have beaten the End, but there's much more to see and do. Where will you go next? What will you build? We can't wait to see.

MARSH DAVIES
THE MOJANG TEAM